A Paean To Deon

by

Wally James Foster

**Grosvenor House
Publishing Limited**

This book is published by
Grosvenor House Publishing Ltd
Link House
140 The Broadway, Tolworth, Surrey, KT6 7HT.
www.grosvenorhousepublishing.co.uk

A CIP record for this book
is available from the British Library

ISBN 978-1-78623-853-5

A PAEAN FOR DEON

My clumsy "thank you" for our very
special love affair. In our marriage,
you brought out the best in all of us.

So many poets: strong inspirations:
God, life, death, nature, passion,
Friends and family love.
If, unwittingly, I plagiarised
I plead forgiveness, 'twas not deliberate.

Elegant Girl

Darling, you stole my life
When first I saw you:
An elegant girl.
Later, I found you
To be serene, kind
And always loving.
How could I escape?
Why would I want to?
You were perfection.

First Date

Tea at Dingles: Hepburn at the Royal.
Then through loose Union Street, past Stonehouse Creek,
Walking to happy childhood, Devonport Park,
Where, much later, we would be remembered.

Staring across the park and up river,
Gazing as blazing sun westward sank,
Silent as stones, engendered by innocence,
Still as statues, we could not breathe or speak.

And then, to have you home by ten, we walked,
Still silent, but with hands shyly clasped.
Cheeks brushed in a fumbled attempt to kiss.
We had started a lifetime together.

A.H.

Deon pashed on Audrey Hepburn
But as she knew they'd never meet,
Inside the Forum picture house,
She reluctantly chose me.

1954

Deon Cynthia
With Julia
Full of charm
Arm in arm.
Schoolgirl friends
Latest trends
Giggling girls
Swirls and twirls.

Outrageous skirts
Revealing shirts.
Hips a jerking
Modest twerking.
Move to the beat
Feel the heat.
Self-control
Pre rock and roll.

Hm!

We often walked for many miles to reach
Curiously deserted Whitsand Beach.
That day the tide was out. The sand was warm.
I am still haunted by your girlish form.
Magically fairy-like you spun and danced,
By sparkling sunlight and giggles enhanced.
An attempt to catch you 'twas not to be.
You laughed and quickly ran to the sea.

It was only Spring and the sea still cold,
Surprised, you shrieked and ran for me to hold.
Splashing, we slipped and fell, holding our breath,
Possible passion met an icy death.
Feeling rather foolish in our wet clothes:
"Next time we'd better take them off," I said.
"Hm!" you said, though probably wondered, "why?"

First Walks

On our first gentle walks, a deep love grew,
Nurtured by the sweet heathers, warm zephyrs
And sparkling waves swirling on golden sands
Of our so secret Rame Peninsula.

Like the seasons, our love had highs and lows
And often the uncertainties of youth
Led to hot strife and brief separations
But each time love returned as did Rame Head.

We sometimes stood before the dark altar
Of ancient Saint Germanus's, Rame Church,
Still candlelit after eight centuries,
Ghosted by serfs and their scrimping masters.
Saint Michael's Chapel beckoned us to lunch
Once shade-seeking sheep had been shooed out.

Happy Teens

Way out at sea, no ghostly sailing ship
Leaves for empirical discovery.
No sailing ship returns with stolen bounty
And decimated crew with strange disease.
Drake, Raleigh, Cook and Frenchie Bonaparte
Leaving, homing, off to imprisonment.
My sea dreams are closer to the present.

Before children and responsibility
We sailed on Plymouth Sound to Cawsand Bay.
With help of Cornish locals, baring flesh,
Our dinghy was beached, just below the pub,
Where we quaffed pints of bitter. Yo! Ho! Ho!
This is a memory I well recall.

The Kiss

Without your loving care throughout our years
What would I have been; a useless creature
Wandering the world shedding futile tears,
Hoping that somewhere I'd find a teacher
To guide me on the path to happiness:
A path where at the end there shone a light
Which promised love and sweet caress.
Too soon that light dimmed and darkness brought night.

But there'd been a kiss that shuddered my life,
A passionate kiss, with my future wife,
Both fierce and gentle, a deep mystery,
The product of secret sweet sorcery.
What would we have been without that first kiss
Bringing us loving eternal bliss.

Dream Of The Past

What would my entirety have achieved
Had I not met and loved you true.
My first and only darling; my love grew
But, with foresight, I would have ever grieved.

Because you made me what I am this day
It is easier to cope with loss
But still I wish I could have borne your cross
So you'd have stayed and for us all would pray.

In my constant waking dream you bring:
The girl with her friend walking past the church;
The girl at school I coached to run and sing;
The young wife who learnt much and helped me search;
The mother and grandma, loving and kind;
You stepping with dignity, your God to find.

1967

The Germans just didn't get it:
They just didn't understand,
Never stepping from the safe path
On post-church forest walks.
They always wore their best clothes,
Often bought thirty years before;
No bratwurst, hot or cold drinks,
But leather handbags clutched instead,
They picked their way past the British
Lounging on warm dry forest ferns.

Whilst German children looked amazed,
British boys and girls screeched about;
A gentle kind of hunter
Searching out their Easter Eggs.
Cautiously a German girl
Received a tiny gold-foiled egg
From a grubby British hand and then,
Concerned that she had left the path,
She turned and scurried swiftly back.

Both groups of parents shyly smiled,
A sign of friendship after strife.

A Memory of a drive from Netheravon to Marlborough

Since you followed your Angel on the path
Danced by those who have avoided God's wrath,
In case you should have chosen here to roam
There have been flowers in your earthly home.
Oft I visit your place in the Woodland,
A flower from home in my hand;
Last week the final daffodil of Spring
And this, a red rose served heartache to bring.

Morning, fifty-five years ago in Spring
You call from the passenger seat: "Darling!"
A screeching stop brought such a wondrous sight
As snowdropped valley shone in morning light.
Now when I espy a snowdrop haven
It recalls our life close by the Avon.

Stonehenge

After a little thought I give you this:
I will select a moment from my heart.
On Salisbury Plain, twelve houses set apart.
The boys were home and we did kiss.

A consensus said "Stonehenge for cricket."
A time before the fence to keep us out
So we picnicked in the stones without doubt;
We needed no stumps: a stone was a wicket.

At dusk we often played there with our boys,
They certainly preferred it to their toys.
One night, near Midsummer Solstice, we left
A Summer mess-ball and with driving deft
Saw the Henge's shadows drawn their longest.
Despite mess-kit, love was at its strongest.

Firework Competition

A solitary bang
And the pageant begins.
The seaward lights of ships
And beckoning buoys
Pale into candle flame
Against the soaring lights.
Spectators marvel at gold,
Red, Green and even Blue
Exploded annually,
Skywards from Mountbatten Pier,
Especially for us.

Home at Dawn

In warm sunshine, standing over the grave
Of that lithe dancing girl from long ago,
Thoughts drifted. A private German Kellar
Where she was the girl to whom the Regiment's
Callow subalterns and naughty majors
Paid court but expected only one dance.
As the Sun rose, walking home, hands clasped,
Dancing forgotten; a mother's duty called.
From the moment that the Angel took her
My dancing girl is ever on my mind.

Crescent Moon

High tide, Diana's crescent moon
And the glory of a sunset
Blue, green and orange in the west.

A simple man cannot believe
Greater beauty exists elsewhere.

Horizon far, black clouds inch up
Warning us that glories have an end
And every end must take its turn.

Dreaming

I need a garden where our souls can meet:
A tiny Owl Cottage with natural plants.
Snowdrops will herald the triumph of Spring.
Along with ever present primroses;
Daffodils, narcissi and simple tulips
Will follow but daisies and buttercups
Chase close, claiming their rightful yearly place.

Irony

As we tidied and threw out old farm junk
So the adders and grass snakes departed
Away from our attempts to replicate
Paradise in Owl Cottage's garden.

The pond we made brought frog, newt and toad,
Wild orchids and Nature's pretty flowers.
Herons and wild duck came, never nesting.
Once we saw a long sinuous adder
Snake across the water perhaps to scare
The baby grass snakes 'neith a piece of pot.

Owl Cottage Pond at Owl Call, entrancing
As Venice and wild as Africa's Cape
So we were happy not to travel and
We listened and watched but night came too soon.

Owl Garden

At the bottom of our acre, where drops
Steeply the valley to the River Yealm,
We sat on balmy Summer evenings
And watched the glorious setting sun.
The bats still circle hawthorns and great oaks,
While owls swoop Yonge's Field, sometimes
  snatching prey.
Rabbits hug the hedgerows venturing out
To test the defences of the veggie patch.
Your sweet Bantams have not been replaced
So pheasants will work harder for their grain.
Sometimes a fox, pretending not to care,
Seeing pheasants and rabbits escaping,
Will trot past in pursuit of who knows what.
My reveries have us sitting on our bench
Watching Ben and Amelia prodding
The bonfire into dense smoke then bright flame:
An age gap stopped them playing together
But now it's difficult to separate the two
And in spirit I see them joyously
Dancing under Grandma's tender care.

Owl Cottage Bedtime

Gwanma's in the kitchen
Baking chocolate cakes that
I mixed a while ago
And while they are cooking
We'll play a game of chase.

Now that it is bath time
She's washing off the mud
And I'll wriggle and giggle
As she raspberries my tummy
And puts my jammies on,
Calling out to Grandpa
"We're ready, Darling, now!"

Pops then will read to me
And I will go to sleep.

Milly and Livy

Milly and Livy, close friends forever
In Summer-time play on the garden lawns,
Dancing fairies floating in water spray.
After walking through cornfields
And playing pooh sticks in the Yealm,
Giggling teatime in the cherry tree tent,
From Omil's Cafe. Oh to be seven again.

Owl Garden

I daydream of the Copper Beach,
Growing lofty in Owl Garden,
A loving gift from our three sons.
In more blissful dreamy times
It offered shade to planted ferns
And informal Summer suppers.

My thoughts inexorably lead
Through the old oak ivied gateway
To Owl's natural fern garden
Which even now whispers to me:
"We will be here, when you have gone,
Keeping your dreams for those to come."

Millie and Ben's flagged hedge-treehouse
Will by now have rotted away,
With remains burnt on Spring's bonfire
And quickly replaced by Nature.

Inspired by Owl Garden

I need a country garden
In which your favourite flowers
Grow in Nature's sequences.
Snowdrops will play hide-and-seek
In late snow but always win,
Glistening with ice, diamond
Beauty sparkling in sunlight.
Following careful planting
The thrusting daffodil hosts
Will shoot quickly, reminding gardeners
With noisy machines, to stay away.
The barren pond will stir.
Flag iris indicate intention
And annoying gunnera lose
First shoots to frosts but
Recover, ready for their late Summer
Charge to giant-conceiling height.
Summer roses will flower
Red, white and yellow
Single and in clusters
Some struggling into
Late December.
Primroses will bloom all the year,
Solitary winter flowers
Joined by thousands into
Late Spring and Summer.

Bird Seed

Dim, dozy denizen of Owl Cottage,
Evie Cat, lies sleepy in the garden,
Defying cross birds and mouse, twitching tail
In irritation at the chirping din.

Birds, but not mouse, lose natural fear
And choose to ignore the one watchful eye
Which slowly loses interest and closes.
Chirpy birds and tired cat in harmony.

Owl Cottage Pond

The Summer before you left,
For the first time in fourteen years
By the pond, left natural
For such eventualities
Came the orchids: Bee and March.
The summer before you left.

Winter Cat

As the sun drops, snowdrops shiver,
All about the garden quiver.
Beautiful though as Winter be
The Cottage calls for you and me,
Where log fire, fed by dead oak trees,
Warms sleepy cat upon your knees.

Precious

Dry and dusty is my favourite possession.
The lavender that you picked and entwined,
On our last slow journey round Owl Cottage's
Peaceful gardens, is now a reminder
Of our time of love in that precious place.

Owl Cottage is Burning Down

Phones here, Phones there,
Owl Cottage is Burning Down.
Some see the smoke from miles away
Owl Cottage is Burning Down.
First the flood, then the fire
Owl Cottage is Burning Down.
The thatch has gone, the roof beams too
Owl Cottage is Burning Down.
Twelve appliances so I'm told
Owl Cottage is Burning Down.
Pumping water from the River Yealm
Owl Cottage is Burning Down
Twelve hours later it was gone
Owl Cottage has Burnt Down.
As it's listed it will rise again:
Owl Cottage will be a home again.

Primroses at Christmas

Two leaves denote a primrose
Sacrosanct in the chippings
Safe from plodding boots quite close.
Buds beating the Swallow's wings,
Will quickly turn to flowers,
Lasting, perhaps, 'til bells ring
And Christmas choirs do sing.

The Footpath

The footpath by the water's edge
Passes below my windows,
Gently busy but never crowded,
Except for annual firework nights.
It leads to work, to school
And the Barbican's pleasures.
Solitary girls clopping to meetings
That will change, forever, their lives,
Remind me of you.
Boys and girls in pairs just
Wandering and wondering the future,
Remind me of us.
Couples with children, tight little units,
Luckily not knowing the future,
Remind me of us.
Couples old in body, young at heart,
Loving and leading grandchildren,
Remind me of us.

Though we never walked the path together,
I see our life together reflected
By all who pass my windows,
Reminding me of us.

Fishing Boats

Under the warm ambient lights,
Fishing boats daily leave their safe haven,
Red and green bobbing lights soon vanishing
Into night's seemingly stygian darkness.
Unlike Man on his final star journey,
They will return.

Town Birds

Each night the blackbird and his mate
Choose balconies to serenade
The Western Sun before it sinks
And like their Owl Cottage cousins
Fall silent when the Orb has gone.

Plymouth Sound

Disturbing fish and crabs from sandy sleep
Ghostly bones squirm in the turbulent deep
When clawing for long departed souls
Risen centuries past through bloody shoals.

Ancient fishermen from shore and dugout,
Sailors released from discipline and knout
Cut down by Death's all consuming scythe
Doomed for Eternity to groan and writhe.

Use of new techniques and diving skills
Enhance the treasure hunter's well earned thrills
As Roman pots and shards, to be rebuilt,
Are teased by hand from silent shifting silt.

Nuclear

The sun has westward sunk
Against a pink-green sky.
Nagasakis of clouds
Drift high above the Bay.
Eddystone twinkleless:
Perhaps the end has come.

To Men

Never pass the chance to show affection
Nor miss a chance to kiss one you adore.
Show your love with sweet touches and soft words.
Gentle her in all things as oft you can,
For one day, staring at an empty space,
You'll wonder if you really showed your love.

Pathway

From birth we tread the path set by our Lord
Blinded that it leads us to our last breath:
Madness would consume should mankind laud
The inevitability of death.
So we hide in the beauty of God's world
Seeing and hearing only sights and sounds
Which protect us from thoughts of an underworld,
'Til we are placed beneath our grassy mounds.

The world's complexity is far too great
For Man's feeble intellect to perceive,
So better not to dither and debate,
The Judgement Day, with those who disbelieve.
Just enjoy the world for all that it is
And thank the Lord who shares all that is His.

Seasons

The promise of Summer's viridity
Leads quietly into Autumnal decline,
Reminding us that continuity
Is but sunshine changed to moon and star shine.

We are lulled by Autumn's gloriousness:
As red, yellow, bronze bring beauteous sight
Soon lapsing into depressing blackness,
Foreshadowing a cruel eternal night.

How redolent of Mankind's fate is this.
We will take our final fall in Winter,
Plunging deep into infinite abyss,
With the last step of a blind death walker
But with God offering love unceasing
All who accept his hand will rise in Spring.

Disbelief

Before the Age of Disbelief
In some naive Old Master works
There lies the lazy form of God
Hovering light upon a cloud.
An unsmiling bearded image
Scowling at bearded mortal men,
Going about Old Testament
Lore of judging fellow men
Pushing them towards eternal Hell.

My God is He who was revealed
In the lifetime of Jesus Christ,
Who would smile kindly at the thought
That Man should try to understand
The unsolvable mystery
That is the Holy Trinity

Ten million priests have tried and failed,
What is the point of trying more.
Point us to acts of charity
And let our kind God show us pity.

In Love Again

Darling, in your heaven, you know all things:
You know I have fallen madly in love.
She is not a seductress turtle dove
But she steals my heart when she sings.

Compelling dark brown eyes and light brown hue
The so perfect legs, quite miraculous.
She comes to my table and makes no fuss.
The moment is perfect for lovers two.

It all started with a chocolate cake
And then 'twas only gold she'd want and take,
Pecking golden sugar from outstretched hand.
I thought I'd test her love with proffered sand
But away she flew, leaving me so blue.
Darling, I know you'd love my sparrow too.

Yealmpton Woodland Burial

Sunrise and sunsets will bathe us both
When eagerly I join you in your place.
Such a beautiful space for us to troth.
'Twill then be our place and they'll seek our trace,
A stone hidden by grasses, flowers and trees.
I hope they'll come at Summer sunset hush
When all is still and at its silent best:
The silence of the birds precedes the rush
Of scarlet Sun below the Cornish hills.

Man departs and leaves Woodland Burial
To darkness, nature and its denizens.

Perhaps ghosts will dance,
As souls soar skyward.

Ghosts

Across the Yealm
And up the fields
Church bells do ring
To Woodland Trust.
Imprisoned souls
Come out to dance.

We cannot touch.
We cannot see.
We cannot speak.
We are but dust.
Dust collapses
And we are gone.

Our Place

Cloud-clear days and nights,
When the Sun and Moon
Shine on us both,
You in your place
And me in mine,
Even more I yearn
To be with you
At peace in earth.

Love

What can heal a broken heart:
What can ever reassure
Knowing that we are apart
Not just now but evermore?

We become the gentle breeze
That moves the meadow flower
Fluttering about to tease
Or we dwell in ashy bower.

Grass

Perhaps the grass and plants
I clear by hand
From your tiny plot
Are already influenced
By your nearby ashes
And if so, I wish
To be grass with you.

Silence

Though numerous, the skylarks are unseen
But we hear their heavenly evensong
Ringing across the meadow, down the dene,
Crescendoing 'til silence reigns nightlong.

Now all birds are quiet, save for the owl
Swooping, eerily crying o'er a grave,
Hunting prey disturbed by a fox on the prowl.
In earth silent dead lie in their enclave.

You too are there and just like the skylark
Are now seen only in my memory
But I hear your voice whisper through the dark,
Sound advice giving me the boundary,
Within which I should live my shortening life,
Guiding those you still love, away from strife.

Written at Woodland

Blues, whites, yellows
At your grave;
Reminders of how much
You loved God's gifts.

Snowdrops, bluebells
And primroses,
God's annual gifts.
Reminders that
Should Man destroy
Himself, a flower
Will struggle through.

Woodland Burial

Icy starlight washes dark earth to life
But fails to stir the gem to earth returned.
Nature's beauty just a sad memory
For those who shared deepest love.

Two Hundred Dreams to Woodland

Is that you standing by my tree?
Why do you often visit me?
Oh! So you want my thoughts today.
Silly! You only have to say.
Imagine I'm a distant star.
Thought of disport quite exquisite
Will leave you no need to visit.
Sadly you know I cannot speak
The words that desperately you seek.
Why do you stand above my ground?
Join me and share the peace I've found.

Woodland

At Woodlands, first light, early morning dew
Wakes and nourishes newly planted yew.
Damp rabbits skitter-scatter, on wet ground,
In panic to their burrows; safety found.
It is the earliest that I've come to you,
Needing to tell you that my love is true.
And in remembrance of your perfect grace,
I long to join you in our last embrace.

A Woodland Talk

There is a path on which I walk
A frequent walk for us to talk.
Sometimes the sun; sometimes the rain
It is the land where you do reign.

Today the bells ring up the dene
You whisper softly what they mean.
They are telling that some day soon
I'll lie with you 'neith Sun and Moon.

Dabbling Stream

I dabbled in the Wolf Cubs, the Boy Scouts too.
I dabbled with the keyboard, the clarinet too.
I dabbled on the rugby pitch, the cricket pitch too.
I found Darling Deon and dabbled with love.

As a girl you dabbled on a pony, feeding farm stock
    too.
You dabbled as a carer, when your mother was ill.
You dabbled in the Red Cross and as a senior girl too.
You were a very special girl and dabbled rather well.
We dabbled then together and had three boys.

Together we dabbled in the Navy, the Army too.
We dabbled with antiques and rare books too.
We dabbled with estate agency and teaching too.
We renovated, bought and sold houses too.
We dabbled with retirement, twenty blissful years.
We dabbled with Owl Cottage and gardening too.

You were so very beautiful, but now you've gone
So I dabble with my memory to bring you back.
Our whole life was a dabble, trying this and that,
Everything we dabbled in was joyous in extreme:
We found that if you dabbled, Love came too.

Star Express

Just because you are gone from here
I have not stopped loving you.
There are a few things to be done
Before I take the Star Express.
Soon those we loved so dearly
Will join our flight and no one
Will remember our time on Earth.

Moment of Magic

This is a moment when the Western sky
Is unutterably beautiful and
As at Owl Cottage, my heart longs to share.
For a moment or two you'd drop your tools
And rushing to catch the magic instant,
We would stand entranced and, perhaps because
We moved towards the inevitable end,
Unseen tears would bring us even closer.

Safe

Darling, we have missed the safe harbourage
Provided by your sweet serenity.
You, through red and green of crowded anchorage,
Calmly captained us to life's sheltered havens,
Where contrary tides and mighty storms
Could not plunge us to the depths.

Zephyrus

Today, Zephyrus gentles past,
The balcony on which I dream,
Passing through Mountbatten mast
Then on across the Yealmpton stream
And up the valley to Woodland,
Where your ashes are moulded by God's Hand.
If I could travel with the wind
I would happily my life exscind.

Deon

The tenderest of poesy cannot convey
How much our hearts will continue to ache.
For you, whose soul soared so swiftly away,
Our tears come through dreams and when we awake.

Never to see, hear or touch you again,
Nor sit together as day turns to eve,
Not to walk golden field or verdant lane
Are cruel concepts that we cannot believe.

The depths of love we have for you
Is measured in memories, sad but blest.
Our tears, early morning and evening dew,
Nourish garden rose and Nature's own best.
There are times when we suffer loneliness
And 'tis then we most crave your loveliness.

Dream of the Past

What would my entirety have achieved
Had I not met and loved you true.
My first and only darling; my love grew
But, with foresight, I would have ever grieved.

Because you made me what I am this day
It is easier to cope with my loss
But still I wish I could have borne your cross
So you'd have stayed and for us all would pray.

In my constant waking dream you bring:
The girl with her friend walking past the church;
The girl at school I coached to run and sing;
The young wife who learnt much and helped me search;
The mother and grandma, loving and kind;
You stepping with dignity, your God to find.

Love

Knowing that one of us was soon to go
Our love and gentleness intensified.
As well as fear we found great joy and so
It continued until the day you died.
Even now our deep and growing love
Continues and soon we'll meet again, above.

Sad Love

Never again will you and I
Walk, holding hands, in the evening's gloom.
Never again will we espy
Nature's beauty in bud and bloom.
Never again will you and I
Kiss as the Sun leaves the Sky.

Deon

We were ordinary people
But, in my eyes, you were the best
A man could ever wish for.

We love our muse, Deon,
And cannot set you free.
We will not let cruel time
Drag you away from us.
Our memories will hold
And keep you all times safe,
While you look down on us:
Loving eternally.

You

I picture you:
I think of you
A thousand times
Each day.

What makes me think
Of Fair Deon:

Our family, friends
Who shared our love,
Sighting a house
Which you'd have loved.
Most flowers,
Music sweet,
And trees; and birds,
God's Universe.

These bring me tears,
Of Sadness
Or Happiness;
I know not which.

From You to Me

I am but ashes.
The heat has gone:
Our passion lost.
I cannot hear.
Though flowers do bloom
I cannot smell:
I cannot see.

Though you do stand
At my cold grave
You must still smile
And care for those
That I did love
And you do love.

Roses

White for purity.
Red for passion.
Yellow for joy.
These will suffice.

Every week without fail
Ten roses I purchase
Of which, two, I take
To your woodland home.
The rest sojourn
On my writing desk,
A constant reminder
Of your love of nature.

They seem to die
At separate rate
And are removed
Like mankind
One by one,
Until the end
Demands renewal.

Swift Time

Both living, every day we said "I love you."
Oh, that we could have our time once more
And, once again, daily say: "I love you"
And love you I do and will forever.
'Tis only since you left, I've understood
The preciousness of time.
Life is short and eternity so long.

Apple Blossom

Next year, perhaps
I'll see the apple blossom,
The leaves, the new and rotting fruit.
One year, for certain.
I'll miss it all,
But then I'll be with you.

Contradiction

In my dreams both night and day,
Your beauty drifts before my eyes
But then so sadly swirls away
Leaving cruel heartache and sighs.

Sweet girl, sacred memory,
Calming my every day and night;
Ivy entwining old oak tree,
You and I, still bound so tight.

Inevitability

As we held you closely to your last breath,
Did you see the Angel's form and beyond?
We pray he was radiant and not in black.
Oh that your last fears in that dread moment
Could have been passed. I would have taken them
But our turn will come and soon we will know.

Love You Too

After you lost the hard struggle to stay,
Presented to us in St. Luke's Chapel,
It didn't look as if you'd gone away.
In farewell you looked so young and peaceful.

But lips that always kissed with purity
Were cooling, soon to be cold as the grave.
Or Shakespeare's "icy lips of Chastity."
Your haunting peacefulness does me enslave.

To The Family and Friends

Do not mourn us
When we have gone;
Rather rejoice
That we were friends
And family.
You must finish
All we started
And left undone.
But above all
You must find love
As deep as ours
Who are now joined
Eternally.
In our final
Flight through stars.

I am fine

Please don't ask me how I am
Or how I feel today.
In the company of family and friends
I am fine.
When I'm alone with she I loved
I am fine.

But often the enormity
Of her physical absence
Strikes my heart and brings tears.
Then I wouldn't tell you
How I feel
So please don't ask me how I am
Or how I feel today.

Owl Primroses

Primroses seeded by nature
Attack Deon's Spring planting.
Granted dispensation by her,
Some remain 'til Winter's icing.

Woodland

Ethereal woodland flowers
Flutter in Summer's warm winds
But fall as Winter's storms bring sleep
Joining you in slumber deep.

Early Summer

Another year has passed and in
Our hedgerows the whites and yellows
Of early Spring have been replaced
With Summer drifts of white-pink-blue.
How my heart aches, for ne'er again
Will we share the joys they bring.

What We Are

Oh: How we have missed the safe anchorage,
Provided by your sweet serenity.
You, the reds and greens of our short voyage,
Made us what we are and wish now to be.

Life Beyond the Grave

You know the secrets of my soul
And now you know the great Unknown
Else there is nothing but the grave.

Until

The sigh that comes a thousand times a day
The heart that aches no matter what is done
The tear that forms and then is brushed away
Will carry on 'til you and I are one.

Patience

Fairish brown to grey
Our love went all the way.
Though our bodies altered
Our love never faltered.
Beneath a woodland tree
I know you wait for me

Epigram

The gentlest of women; where are you now?
Christian God or woodland haunting place will know.

The Beginning

As honest love will constant be,
The future's safe for you and me.
On our flight to Eternity,
We'll meet again and then will see
The path approved by God's assent,
Which will bring us great content.

Inevitability

I try to write
About other things
But always come back
To you.

Punishment

Write "ad infinitum:"
"Cannot live without you."

Reflection

Just one calm sunny instant
But what a moment it was.
You brought warm peace and joy
To all you knew and loved.

Gentlest, Dreamy, Deepest Love

Darling, come gently to me in my dreams:
Once more remind me how your lips did kiss.
Forgive me that I need to ask, it seems
Thankless to forget that which I most miss.

Darling, come gently to me in my dreams
And let me hold you lightly in my arms,
As we softly sigh, until the day's sun beams
Awaken us and you must fly from worldly harms.

Darling, come gently to me in my dreams
And remind me how best to live and love
Family and friends, essentials of our schemes,
Where deepest love was gifted from above.

BIOGRAPHY

Deon and Wally first met, albeit briefly, at St Michael's Church, Plymouth. They were then 14 and 16 years old. They next met when she was a 16 year old Head Girl at Penlee School and he was an 18 year old at Devonport High School undertaking a Teaching practise at Penlee prior to attending St Luke's College, Exeter.

Later a meeting occurred when Deon was at Plymouth Technical College on a secretarial course and Wally was just starting his final year in Exeter: it was September 1956. Wally and his Swansea friend, Bob Ogborne, were walking down Plymouth's Royal Parade and bumped into Deon Badgery and Julia Stevens who were walking up the Parade.

As coffee was, in those days, only for the rich or sophisticates, tea was agreed and we went to the local teashop, a worn Nissen hut, a relic of Plymouth's Blitz.

This was the start of a lifetime journey, perhaps eternal, for Deon and Wally. The earthly part of the journey included over 20 moves.

After a peaceful time spent in the Royal Navy, the Army and attached to the Royal Marines, when his main problem was finding time to play Rugby and Cricket, Wally was invalided out and became Senior Lecturer in charge of 'A' levels at Plymouth College of Further Education. With Deon, he collected and sold 18th century ceramics and antiquarian books and prints from Plymouth's historic Barbican. Deon's main interests were her 3 sons and renovating tired or derelict houses and gardens. She also managed 3 shops.

The Fosters retired some 25 years ago to tend Deon's beautiful Owl Cottage garden in Yealmpton. Deon's love of her sons Jay, Tim and Nick and grandchildren Amelia and Ben was all encompassing welcoming daughters-in-law Lucy and Gillian.

Lightning Source UK Ltd.
Milton Keynes UK
UKOW03f1956070417
298609UK00001B/16/P

9 781786 238535